Princess Flower

by

Hasan Erkek

Translated by
Volga Yılmaz Gümüş

Edited by Gillian Bickley

Supported by
Ministry of Culture and Tourism
of the Republic of Turkey

PRINCESS FLOWER is a charming play suitable for children aged eight and above, with an appropriate and modern message based on a traditional theme and taking about an hour to perform. Originally written in Turkish, it has been performed in Turkey and is in the repertoire of both the State Theatres and the City Theatres of Istanbul. In 2006 it won an award from the following bodies: ASSITEJ (International Association of Theatre for Children and Young People), ITI (International Theatre Institute) and IPF (International Playwrights Forum).

In the mythical Land of Flowers, where people earn their living by growing flowers, the seventeen-year-old Flower Princess, Lily, is waiting for the time of the flower harvest to marry Snapdragon, the Flower Prince. But her mother, Queen Rose, falls and breaks her leg. Her father, King Bluebell, is so upset that he issues a command forbidding women to go out to work anymore. They should stay at home engaged in housework.

Soon all the flowers wither and die and even their seeds are useless. The king talks to the queen about what to do: "I should go to the Land of Giants to get more seeds, but I am old for the journey. If we only had a son, he could go to the Land of Giants for me."

Princess Flower, overhearing this, is hurt. "I can go!" With her parents' consent, so she does, riding her horse, Benny. They have many adventures, meeting creatures whom they help and who help them (a pair of nightingales, a buck and a hind, two white eagles, a female rabbit). Finally, in the Land of Giants, the Flower Princess is told, "If men and women work equally", then the flowers will bloom again.

She returns home with new seeds, given by the King and Queen of the Land of Giants and conveys this message. The king, her father, rescinds his command. Men and women work together again in the flower fields and elsewhere. The princess marries Snapdragon, Prince Flower. Her father makes her Queen (with the consent of the people). The new Queen states that she would like Snapdragon, Prince Flower, to reign with her. There is dancing and rejoicing and the play ends.

Princess Flower

by

Hasan Erkek

Translated
by
Volga Yılmaz Gümüş

Edited by Gillian Bickley

Proverse Hong Kong

Princess Flower
by and © Hasan Erkek, 19 April 2016.
Translated from Turkish by Volga Yılmaz Gümüş
from the original play, *ÇiçekPrenses*, by Hasan Erkek.
2nd pbk edition published in Hong Kong by Proverse Hong Kong,
May 2016 under sole licence.
ISBN: 978-988-8228-41-6
Printed by CreateSpace

1st published in pbk in Hong Kong by Proverse Hong Kong, 19 April 2016
under sole licence.
ISBN 978-988-8228-36-2

Proverse Hong Kong, P. O. Box 259, Tung Chung Post Office, Tung Chung,
Lantau Island, NT, Hong Kong SAR, China.
E-mail: proverse@netvigator.com Web site: www.proversepublishing.com

The right of Hasan Erkek to be identified as the author of this work
has been asserted by him in accordance with
the Copyright, Designs and Patents Act 1988.

Cover design by Proverse Hong Kong and Artist Hong Kong Company.
Front cover image based on a performance poster by RETA Agency, Turkey.
Used with permission.

All rights reserved. No part of this publication may be reproduced, stored in a retrieval system, or transmitted, in any form or by any means, electronic, mechanical, photocopying, recording or otherwise, without the prior written permission of the publisher or publisher and author. The book is sold subject to the condition that it shall not, by way of trade or otherwise, be lent, re-sold, hired out or otherwise circulated without the author's prior written consent in any form of binding or cover other than that in which it is published and without a similar condition including this condition being imposed on the subsequent owner or purchaser. Please contact Proverse Hong Kong (acting as agent for the author) in writing, to request any and all permissions (including but not restricted to republishing, inclusion in anthologies, translation, reading, and use as set pieces in examinations and festivals).
For permission to perform in professional theatres where tickets are sold, please contact the playwright, Hasan Erkek [hasanerkek2012@gmail.com]

**British Library Cataloguing in Publication Data.
A catalogue record for the first edition of this book is available from the British Library.**

INTRODUCTION

Princess Flower represents in a modern form the basic cycle of nature and human life – life, death, and rebirth or renewal – through a collective adventure, blending the fairytale form with that of Turkish ritual village plays and the Turkish national tradition of *karagöz*[1] and *ortaoyunu*.[2]

The play is based on the idea that the female and the male complement each other and indeed are the means by which nature flourishes and birth is achieved.

The king of the country forgets this basic interdependence and separates the work of men and women. Disaster follows. His daughter, Princess Flower, is the means by which the disaster is overcome and an understanding of the king's mistake known.

Acknowledging and reversing his mistake, the old king requests and receives his people's agreement to pass his crown to his daughter, whose public-spirited and successful actions have demonstrated her worthiness for this position. Holding firmly to the hard-won lesson that men and women should work side-by-side, Princess Flower proclaims that she will reign together with her future husband, Prince Flower.

---

[1] The famous Turkish shadow play, where, behind a white screen, semi-transparent puppets made of leather are used to create a shadow effect. The audience, in front of the screen, watch the colourful shadows of the puppets. The two leading characters of these plays are Karagöz and Hacivat. (Translator's Note)

[2] *Ortaoyunu* is a traditional form of theatre, performed mainly in town squares and inns. In some cases, players engage in dialogue with the audience. If we consider the distinction that Bertolt Brecht makes between "dramatic theatre" and "epic theatre", *ortaoyunu* belongs to the category, "epic theatre". Its leading characters, Pişekar and Kavuklu, resemble Hacivat and Karagöz in *karagöz* plays, described above. However, different from *karagöz*, *ortaoyunu* is performed by players in an extremely simple setting. *Ortaoyunu* has lost its popularity over time. (Translator's Note)

An old cycle has ended and a new one is about to begin. The change of ruler, renewed harvest, and the wedding of Princess Flower and Prince Flower are celebrated as the play ends. There is hope for the future.

Dramatic Structure and Mode of Performance
Princess Flower is structured as a Play within a Play in the tradition of village performances. After singing an opening song the players directly announce that they are going to tell a story through performing a play for the audience.

The set and props and some of the costumes are prepared in front of the audience and used minimally. Some characters, for example Benny the Horse, Begonia the Mare, King Giant and Queen Giant are each performed by two players. The Butterfly, Male and Female Nightingales, trapped Buck and anxious Hind, hungry Snake, White Eagle Fledglings, White Eagles and Rabbit are created in front of the audience with a few simple props. The actors themselves put in place the sets for the Great Forest, Fountain, Red Desert and Lofty Mountain, as well as producing the effects, such as howling, wind, rain and lightning. Hand puppets, controlled by the actors who sing their songs, represent the male and female nightingales.

The play uses many elements used in traditional Turkish drama, including the mimes of milking a cow and drinking water from a fountain and the representation of a journey by circling the stage several times.

Modification of Traditional Elements
A Princess
In traditional fairy tales, it is usually a prince who sets out on an adventure to prove himself and/or to achieve some noble outcome to benefit others. But in *Princess Flower*, it is a princess who undertakes the adventure, encountering and overcoming three obstacles, and showing her good qualities of character.

She succeeds, not by exercising physical strength as typically seen in the adventures of male characters but through unpremeditated kindness, generosity, compassion, considerateness, politeness, sense of justice and diplomacy, in other words by using her heart, mind, and conscience.

She passes through the Great Forest with the help of two deer, whom she had helped. She crosses the Red Desert shaded under the wings of two eagles, whose fledglings she had saved from a snake. She surmounts the Lofty Mountain with the help of a rabbit, whom she had helped to cross the desert on her way home.

Giants

Giants and the land of giants are common in fairytales and in the *Karagöz* tradition. In *Princess Flower* they are given a new character and role. They are the source of truth, understanding and renewal. It is from them that Princess Flower seeks the flower-seeds that her country needs if its citizens are to resume their previous productive and contented life, and it is from them that she learns the cause of the recent problem in her country.

In *Princess Flower*, being like a giant refers to wisdom, maturity, enlightenment and alert understanding. This is why, when giving voice to King Giant and Queen Giant – the characters whom the author suggests should be performed by two players, one standing on the shoulders of another – the author makes the player who holds up the other echo the words of the player on top, to proclaim and propagate an aware understanding.

Flower Image

Why has the playwright set this story in a land of flowers? – Undoubtedly because of the many relevant connotations that thoughts of flowers bring: for example, flowering, the re-growth of nature, the renewal of human beings and humanity. It may be suggested that the central character here is a female, not only possibly to show sympathy for the cause of equal rights for women, but to represent fertility.

An Ending Full of Hope and Joy
In ritual plays dedicated to cultivating and harvesting, there are elements such as community sowing and harvesting and collective celebrations by dance and song in response to blessings received. In *Princess Flower*, community actions similarly respond to the action of the play (as the chorus in Greek drama and drama under its influence also does).

At the end of the play, the joyous dancing and singing of the people in response to the renewal of nature merge with the wedding dance of Princess Flower and her Prince. Nature and human beings share both the actuality and the promise of joyous change and renewal. The players in their player identity also dance enthusiastically in a dance recalling the *semah* ritual of whirling dervishes. The feelings of enthusiasm, celebration and blessing flow beyond the stage and into real life with the participation of audience.

The play is a story of new hope, the story of a new generation that is to construct the future.

— Based on an article by **Prof. Dr. Nurhan Tekerek,** 'A fantasy play where traditional elements intermingle with fairytale motifs: The land of flowers and its kind-hearted Princess Flower'

Sivas State Theatre (Turkish National Theater In Sivas Region) (2013-2014)

DIRECTOR
Çağman Pala

CAST
Narrator, Citizen, Female Nightingale, Mother Eagle
Selda Şahin
Narrator, Citizen, Male Nightingale, Cactus
Tansel Aytekin
King Flower, Snake, Father Eagle, Horse
Ömer Eryiğit
Queen Flower, Female Deer, Rabbit, Queen of Giants
Ufuk Bostancı
Princess Flower
Begüm Şahin
Prince Flower, Citizen, Male Deer, Dog, King of Giants
Burçhan Göze
Benny, Citizen
S. Veysel Zurnazanlı
Begonia, Citizen, Tree, Cactus
Zehra Tosun
Citizen, Dwarf Guard, Tree
Arif Özkalay
Citizen, Guard, Tree, Cactus
Belgin Ünlü
Citizen, Dwarf Guard, Tree, Cactus
Gamze Karaca

Istanbul City Theatre, Republic of Turkey (2011-2014)

DIRECTOR
Ece Okay

CAST
Narrator
Elçin Atamgüç
Narrator
Yalçın Avşar
King Flower (King Hyacinth)
Nevzat Çankara
Queen Flower (Queen Rose)
Nazan Yatgın
Princess Flower
Ece Özdikici
Prince Flower (Prince Snapdragon)
Ozan Gözel
Benny the Horse
Ümit Daşdöğen
Begonia the Horse
Senem Oluz

PRINCESS FLOWER
BY HASAN ERKEK

CHARACTERS OF THE EXTERNAL PLAY

1st Player	1st Narrator, Guide; Female
2nd Player	2nd Narrator, Guide; Male
3rd Player	Bluebell, King Flower
4th Player	Rose, Queen Flower
5th Player	Lily, Princess Flower
6th Player	Head of Benny, Male Horse
7th Player	Back of Benny, Male Horse
8th Player	Head of Begonia, Female Horse
9th Player	Back of Begonia, Female Horse
10th Player	Snapdragon, Prince Flower
11th Player	Miscellaneous Roles
12th Player	Miscellaneous Roles
13th Player	Miscellaneous Roles
14th Player	Miscellaneous Roles
15th Player	Miscellaneous Roles
16th Player	Miscellaneous Roles

PRINCESS FLOWER
BY HASAN ERKEK

CHARACTERS OF THE INTERNAL PLAY

LILY	Princess Flower, daughter of the King of the Land of Flowers, 17 years old
SNAPDRAGON	Prince Flower, 18 years old
BLUEBELL	King Flower, King of the Land of Flowers, 60 years old
ROSE	Queen Flower, Queen of the Land of Flowers, 55 years old
BENNY	Lily's Horse
BEGONIA	A mare, Benny's wife
BUCK	Male deer
HIND	Female deer
MALE NIGHTINGALE	
FEMALE NIGHTINGALE	
GRAND SNAKE	Male snake
MALE WHITE EAGLE	
FEMALE WHITE EAGLE	
COTTON RABBIT	
HOUND	
HORSE	
QUEEN OF GIANTS	
KING OF GIANTS	
CITIZENS	Citizens of the Land of Flowers
GUARDS	Guards of the Land of Flowers

PROLOGUE

The materials, costumes and accessories required for staging a play. A musical band on a higher-level platform located at any part of the stage. The PLAYERS enter the stage from various entrances, singing and dancing.

THE PROLOGUE SONG

Hello, hello,
Hello children, hello adults,
Hello the world, hello life,
Hello the rising sun,
Hello the setting moon.

Hello, hello,
Hello theatre, hello stage,
Hello the facts, hello the tales,
Hello the dreams,
Hello the plays.

1st PLAYER	Welcome, children... Welcome, our young friends.
2nd PLAYER	Welcome, adults.
1st PLAYER	We're going to stage a play for you.
2nd PLAYER	Here is our stage. This is our setting.
1st PLAYER	And those are our props.
2nd PLAYER	This is our make-up.
1st PLAYER	We have prepared a fairy-tale drama for you...
2nd PLAYER	A dramatic fairy-tale.
1st PLAYER	We are going to both tell and play.
2nd PLAYER	We are going to both play and tell.
1st PLAYER	Come on, let's cut it short and begin our play.
2nd PLAYER	Yes, let's cut it short and begin our fairy tale. But how shall we begin?
1st PLAYER	Let's begin as all other fairy tales begin. Once upon a time.
2nd PLAYER	Once upon a time there was a very beautiful land in a distant continent.

The other PLAYERS act as stage-hands, putting the set into place, starting to create a representation of the Land of Flowers with flowers made of fabric or paper. The 1st PLAYER and the 2nd PLAYER turn the stage into the Land of Flowers by stringing flowers up along a rope.

1st PLAYER	It was a wonderful land.
2nd PLAYER	It was gorgeous...
1st PLAYER	Very beautiful...
2nd PLAYER	Like a flower...
1st PLAYER	As its name implies, the Land of Flowers.

THE WONDERFUL LAND OF FLOWERS

1st PLAYER   The Land of Flowers had a King. His name was Bluebell. Everybody called him King Flower.

The 3rd PLAYER who plays the role of King gets prepared. The other PLAYERS help him into his costume. Then they take him by the arm and make him stand on a platform to the left backstage.

2nd PLAYER   King Bluebell was a very kind-hearted king.
1st PLAYER   He loved his people very much.
2nd PLAYER   He always worked for their happiness...
1st PLAYER   But he was a little bit old.

The 3rd PLAYER does not change his position. He continues to stand straight.

2nd PLAYER   He was a little bit old... Old... A little bit.

After these words, King Bluebell, who has been standing straight with a youthful appearance, becomes an old king, bending his back slightly. This image of old age is reinforced by makeup and accessories. A PLAYER gives the King his sceptre. The King seems to be standing with the help of his sceptre.

2nd PLAYER   The Land of Flowers had a queen as well.

1st PLAYER   Her name was Rose. Everybody called her Queen Flower.

The other PLAYERS help the 4th PLAYER into the costume of Queen Rose.

2nd PLAYER   She also was very kind-hearted.

Queen Flower moves onto the platform where the King is standing. She takes him by the arm. They freeze.

1st PLAYER   King Flower and Queen Flower had a daughter.
2nd PLAYER   Her name was Lily.
1st PLAYER   But everybody called her Princess Flower.

The 5th PLAYER steps forward. The other PLAYERS help her into her costume. Their mime and gestures support the narration.

1st PLAYER   She was very wise
2nd PLAYER   And very beautiful, Princess Flower.
1st PLAYER   She was very kind-hearted as well...
2nd PLAYER   And she kept the kind-hearted handsome Prince Flower in her kind heart. His name was Snapdragon.

The PLAYER acting as Prince Flower steps forward. He takes Princess Flower by the hand.

1st PLAYER	He was a very kind-hearted prince. Good-natured. Wise. Hard-working.
2nd PLAYER	The flowers that he grew always won first prize in competitions held during the flower harvest.
1st PLAYER	But his most valuable flower was Princess Flower. He was looking forward to getting married to her.
2nd PLAYER	The King and Queen promised that their wedding would take place in the coming flower harvest season. So the young couple were waiting for the flower harvest season impatiently.

Prince Flower gives a bunch of flowers to Princess Flower. He kisses her and steps to one side.

1st PLAYER	She was very kind-hearted, Princess Flower.
2nd PLAYER	She was fond of human beings. She was fond of animals.
1st PLAYER	Princess Flower even talked to animals...
2nd PLAYER	She got along well with animals.

The 6th PLAYER who plays the head of Benny steps forward to draw attention, neighing like a horse. The 7th PLAYER moves as well.

2nd PLAYER	(*Remembers*) Oh, yes, Princess

Flower had a horse.

The 6th PLAYER stands as if he were the head of the horse, wearing a horse mask. The 7th PLAYER bends down to form the back part of the horse. He grasps the waist of the 6th PLAYER. The other PLAYERS help the 6th PLAYER and the 7th PLAYER to put on the costume of a beautiful horse, using some pieces of cloth on which flowers are illustrated. The other players decorate the horse with various accessories.

1st PLAYER	The name of this beautiful horse was Benny.
2nd PLAYER	Benny was a very good-natured, a very kind-hearted horse.
1st PLAYER	He was Princess Flower's best friend.

Princess Flower strokes the neck of the horse.

PRINCESS F.	How are you, my dear Benny?
BENNY	I am fine, dear Princess Flower. But I'd be better if I had some daisy roots and violet leaves to eat. You can't imagine how hungry I am.
PRINCESS F.	Don't worry, Benny. I'll give you plenty of those.
2nd PLAYER	No, the story's not over yet. Benny was a male horse. And he had a wife... A mare. Her name was Begonia.
8th PLAYER (an actress)	We're going to play the role of Begonia. (*She shakes her hair*

	and neighs like a horse. She is wearing the mask of a female horse.)
9th PLAYER (an actress)	Yes, we're going to play her role.

The 8th PLAYER stands as if she were the head of the horse wearing a horse mask. The 9th PLAYER bends down to form the back part of the horse. She grasps the waist of the 8th PLAYER. The other PLAYERS help the 8th PLAYER and the 9th PLAYER to put on the costume of a beautiful horse, decorated with lilies. They decorate the horse with various accessories. The two horses neigh to show their love for each other.

BEGONIA	I love you very much, Benny.
BENNY	I love you very much, too, Begonia. But I also love Princess Flower. I do whatever she wants.
PRINCESS F.	Come on, Benny. Let's go.
BENNY	(*Looking back at Begonia*) OK, let's go... Good-bye Begonia.

Princess Flower and Benny leave the stage in a friendly manner. The PLAYERS who play Begonia leave the role of Begonia and return to their player identity.

2nd PLAYER	The Land of Flowers had citizens, too... Women, men and children like flowers.
1st PLAYER	The people of the Land of Flowers earned their living growing flowers.

The other male and female PLAYERS get prepared to play

the role of the people of the Land of Flowers. They put on miscellaneous costumes and accessories.

2nd PLAYER　　Together they plant miscellaneous flowers in their fields.

The 1st PLAYER and the 2nd PLAYER reinforce the atmosphere of the Land of Flowers with dried or artificial flowers of various colours that they place on the stage.

2nd PLAYER	They used to grow roses, bellflowers...
1st PLAYER	Violets, daffodils...
2nd PLAYER	Daisies, day lilies...
1st PLAYER	Clivias, begonias...
2nd PLAYER	Azaleas, camellias...
1st PLAYER	Water lilies, poppies...
2nd PLAYER	Tulips and orchids.

All male and female citizens of the Land of Flowers take hoes and shovels in their hands. In a choreographed order, they sing as they work in the fields.

THE FLOWER GROWERS' SONG

Let us sow and scatter flower seeds
With our hoes, shovels and hands.
Let us make flowers grow everywhere
By our joy, love and songs.

2nd PLAYER	The citizens of the Land of Flowers gather the flowers they planted...
1st PLAYER	And sell to neighbouring countries fresh flowers, dried flowers...
2nd PLAYER	Flower sugar, flower jam...
1st PLAYER	Flower honey, flower tea...
2nd PLAYER	Flower cookies, flower drinks...
1st PLAYER	Flower scent, flower medication...
2nd PLAYER	And buy salt, sugar, soap, flour...
1st PLAYER	Milk, eggs, butter...
2nd PLAYER	Apples, oranges, peaches...
1st PLAYER	Melons, water melons and bananas for their households...
2nd PLAYER	Nice clothing for themselves...
1st PLAYER	Pretty toys for their children...
2nd PLAYER	And lead merry lives.

The citizens of the Land of Flowers create a hardworking and happy scene. They freeze for a while.

1st PLAYER	One day, a sunny day...
2nd PLAYER	While the flowers were

	gleaming...
1st PLAYER	And the flowery scent spread everywhere..
2nd PLAYER	Queen Flower mounted Begonia...

The other PLAYERS prepare the Horse Begonia. The Queen mounts the horse.

1st PLAYER	And she began to ride among the flower fields.

While the Queen passes among the citizens on her horse, the citizens display their love for her. Queen Flower salutes the people joyfully and enthusiastically.

2nd PLAYER	Just at that moment a flowery butterfly flying joyously settled on the nose of the horse.

The 1st PLAYER places a butterfly, attached to the point of a stick, on the nose of the 8th PLAYER who plays the head of Begonia.

1st PLAYER	Begonia, whose nose itched, forgot that the Queen was on her back.

Begonia neighs, and bucks. The Queen rolls over in a comical manner.

1st PLAYER	The Queen fell down and broke her leg.

The 1st PLAYER and the 2nd PLAYER help the Queen

stand up.

1st PLAYER   Then the Queen started to walk with the help of crutches.

The 2nd PLAYER brings the crutches and a plaster cast from the back of the stage. The Queen places her leg in the plaster cast and uses the crutches to walk. She painfully takes a tour around the stage. King Bluebell looks at her dolefully.

1st PLAYER   King Flower was very upset about what had happened.
2nd PLAYER   And he decided to take measures to prevent such painful accidents in future.
KING F.   (*In theatrical fashion*) Women must not go to the flower fields from now on! They must all stay at home! Only men will go to the flower fields! Be it known by all!

A drum hanging around his neck, the 2nd PLAYER, walking around the stage, reads loudly the edict of the King.

2nd PLAYER   Be it known by all that this is the edict of the King of the Land of Flowers. Only men will work in the flower fields from now on. Women will stay at home. They will deal only with housework. Let it be known by all!

The women put their hoes and shovels aside reluctantly, sadly and even furiously, and go to the rear of the stage. They then engage in housework.

1st PLAYER	Only men grew flowers in the fields after that day. Now there were only men in the fields. They looked at the women dolefully. They worked sadly.
2nd PLAYER	The women stayed at home...
1st PLAYER	They cooked...
2nd PLAYER	They washed the dishes...
1st PLAYER	They cleaned their houses...
2nd PLAYER	They made flower jam and flower cookies...
1st PLAYER	They yearned to grow flowers.

The women deal with the above-mentioned housework in choreographed order at one side of the stage. The men supposedly go on working in flower fields at the other side of the stage.

BAD NEWS IN THE LAND OF FLOWERS

1st PLAYER   Without warning, something evil hit the country while the citizens were striving to live their lives as usual.
2nd PLAYER   Something evil hit the country.

The male citizens gather at one side of the stage as if they had gathered to lament over a disaster. Hearing the bad news, the female citizens join them as well.

1st PLAYER   Heeeeyy!
2nd CITIZEN   Ohhhhh!
3rd CITIZEN   Nooooo!
4th CITIZEN   Hmmmm!
5th CITIZEN   Owwww!
6th CITIZEN   Really?!

The citizens look at the ground in surprise. Their mouths are open in wonder and fear. They freeze as if in a photograph.

1st PLAYER   The citizens could not believe their eyes. The colourful flowers that they had sown and grown diligently were drying up.

While narrating, the 1st PLAYER and the 2nd PLAYER start to remove the flowers hanging on the ropes as well as the ropes themselves. They try to create an atmosphere of poverty and disaster.

2nd PLAYER	Roses, bellflowers...
1st PLAYER	Violets, daffodils...
2nd PLAYER	Daisies, day lilies...
1st PLAYER	Clivias, begonias...
2nd PLAYER	Azaleas, camellias...
2nd PLAYER	Water lilies, poppies...
1st PLAYER	Tulips and orchids... They all... They have all dried up.
1st PLAYER	A malady has dried up all the flowers. We don't know what it is, or where it has come from.

The citizens sit on the floor in despair. They sing an elegiac melody.

CITIZENS	Our land has dried up, we have lost all our flowers. Our hopes have dried up, we have lost all our hope. We are left high and dry. Our hopes have dried up, we have lost all our hope.

They stand motionless.

2nd PLAYER	All of a sudden, the Land of Flowers turned into a wasteland.
1st PLAYER	There were no flowers left.
2nd PLAYER	No seeds to grow more flowers.
1st PLAYER	The Flower citizens were without a remedy.
2nd PLAYER	They did not know what to do.
1st PLAYER	There was no flower harvest, since

2nd PLAYER	there were no flowers. Princess Flower and Prince Flower could not get married because there was no flower harvest.
1st PLAYER	They were unhappy and moody.

Princess Flower and Prince Flower walk through the stage hand in hand, unhappily, their heads bowed.

2nd PLAYER	The Flower citizens searched for a remedy.
1st PLAYER	In the end...

The PLAYERS start to act. We hear the murmurs of the citizens. Then they organize themselves and walk towards the King. Seeing the crowd, the 1st PLAYER and the 2nd PLAYER put on guards' helmets and pick up guards' lances, and stand facing the citizens. The guards obstruct the citizens who try insistently to enter the palace. The citizens start to shout. The King, who has been motionless, begins to move, hears the voices and wonders what has been happening outside.

1st CITIZEN	We want to see our King Flower!
2nd CITIZEN	We want to see our King Bluebell!
3rd CITIZEN	Let us see Our King Bluebell!
4th CITIZEN	We want to see our King Flower!
1st GUARD	Be calm, Flower Citizens!
2nd GUARD	Flower Citizens, please, be quiet!
1st GUARD	Just a moment, Flower Citizens!
1st CITIZEN	We want to see our King Flower!
6th CITIZEN	We want to go to our King Flower!

The King raises his hand. The guards step aside to make way for the King.

KING F.   Let them come! Let my people come here!

The citizens come up to the platform on which the King stands.

EVERYONE   Long live our King! Long live our King Flower Bluebell! Long live our King! May he live long!
KING F.   My dear flower citizens! What has forced you to gather in front of my palace? What is the problem?
1st CITIZEN   Your Majesty, King Flower, our unhappiness deepens day by day...
2nd CITIZEN   Our troubles and problems mount up...
3rd CITIZEN   We are worried...
4th CITIZEN   Our citizens are weary...
5th CITIZEN   Our children are uneasy.
KING F.   The unhappiness of my Flower citizens is my unhappiness. If you weep once, I weep a thousand times. Tell me about your trouble, tell me your problem. I'm listening to you.
4th CITIZEN   You know our problem, Your Majesty, King Flower. Our problem is the malady of our flowers.
2nd CITIZEN   The malady has dried up all our flowers.
1st CITIZEN   We can't grow any flowers.

4th CITIZEN	Our bees can't make flower honey.
2nd CITIZEN	We can't produce flower jam, flower medication, flower scents.
3rd CITIZEN	We can't produce or sell anything.
4th CITIZEN	We can't buy sugar; we can't buy salt and we can't buy flour.
1st CITIZEN	We can't buy milk; we can't buy butter and we can't buy eggs...
5th CITIZEN	New clothes...
2nd CITIZEN	Toys for our children...
1st CITIZEN	No nice paints...
3rd CITIZEN	No lovely dolls or colourful balloons...
4th CITIZEN	Wooden horses, pretty toy propellers...
5th CITIZEN	We can't present flowers to our wives or friends any more...
4th CITIZEN	Our children can't present flowers to their teachers or parents...
3rd CITIZEN	We celebrate our birthdays, anniversaries, and festivals without flowers.
5th CITIZEN	Our Land of Flowers is like a wasteland now...
1st CITIZEN	Flowerless, colourless...
2nd CITIZEN	Colourless, joyless...
3rd CITIZEN	Joyless, scentless.

They bend their heads sorrowfully.

KING F.	My dear Flower Citizens! I know all you have just told me. And I am as worried as you. But I

believe in you, my Flower Citizens. We can overcome all these problems. We can adorn our Land of Flowers with flowers again. We can plant colourful flowers and we can grow colourful flowers again.

Princess Flower walks towards her father. She stands near him and waits to see what is to happen next.

1st CITIZEN	That is why we came here to see you, our King Flower.
3rd CITIZEN	We don't have any seeds to grow new flowers.
1st CITIZEN	We couldn't gather flower seeds to sow new flowers because that pitiless malady has dried up all our flowers.
2nd CITIZEN	We couldn't gather and store the seeds.
5th CITIZEN	We're here to ask for flower seeds from you.
2nd CITIZEN	Please, find us flower seeds so that we can sow new flowers.
3rd CITIZEN	Please, find us flower seeds so that we can grow new flowers.

The King raises his hands to calm the citizens.

KING F.	My dear Flower Citizens. I'll find a remedy for your problem. I'll solve your problem.

Everybody applauds and cheers.

KING F. You know that all the flower seeds are in the Land of Giants. But, as the King of the Land of Flowers, I will find a way of getting you the flower seeds. We'll produce flowers again! We'll be the Land of Flowers again, I promise you.

EVERYONE (*Excitedly and hopefully*) Long live our King Flower! Long live our King! May he live long! May he live long!

Having received the king's promise, the citizens are persuaded and consoled, and they leave the palace. They go to the rear of the stage and revert to their original roles. The 1st PLAYER and the 2nd PLAYER take off their guards' costumes, and revert to their original roles.

1st PLAYER The promise of King Flower has relieved the Flower Citizens.
2nd PLAYER They leave the palace with peace of mind.
1st PLAYER They start to wait impatiently for the day when the King will find them flower seeds.
2nd PLAYER Meanwhile, the King and the Queen start to brood over what to do.

The King and the Queen discuss the problem. Princess Lily reads a book with a flowery cover.

QUEEN F.	Will you go to the Land of Giants?
KING F.	(*Desperately*) I have to go. I have to go because I'm the king of this country.
QUEEN F.	But how will you go? The Land of Giants is very distant.
KING F.	You're right. I am old. I am not strong enough. My eyes aren't as sharp as they used to be. I can't ride well any more.
QUEEN F.	You surely can't overcome all those obstacles.
KING F.	But our flower citizens can't sow flowers if I don't go.
QUEEN F.	You're right. If you don't go, our people will be poor and unhappy...
KING F.	Our Land of Flowers will continue a wasteland...
QUEEN F.	It will have lost all its colours and scent.
KING F.	How painful it is to be the unhappy king of such a country. If only we had a young son...
QUEEN F.	If only we had a wise and strong prince...
KING F.	He would go to the Land of Giants instead of me.
QUEEN F.	If only. He could bring us flower seeds.
KING F.	But we don't have a son. We have a daughter. We're desperate.

Princess Flower stands up and comes up to them.

PRINCESS F.	(*Sadly*) My dear mother, my dear father.
QUEEN F.	Oh, my dear Princess Flower, have you been here all along?
PRINCESS F.	Yes, I accidentally heard all you said.
QUEEN F.	(*Anxiously*) Really?
KING F.	(*Anxiously*) Really?
PRINCESS F.	I'm hurt. Your words have hurt me very much.
QUEEN F.	But what we said has nothing to do with you. We love you very much.
KING F.	But if only you had a brother. He would go to the Land of Giants and bring back the flower seeds we need.
PRINCESS F.	I also can do it, father.
KING F.	Yes, but... But you're a girl.
QUEEN F.	You're too weak to manage it.
PRINCESS F.	Whenever I attempt to do something, you say, "Yes, but you're a girl." But I can do many things that men can do.
KING F.	But....
PRINCESS F.	I have the qualities required for it. I have enough knowledge about life, about human beings and about animals. That's why I can go to the Land of Giants and bring back

	flower seeds.
KING F.	No, no. I can't accept this risk.
PRINCESS F.	Please, let me go, Father. I'm seventeen years old. I'd like to undertake difficult tasks.
KING F.	But the way to the Land of Giants is full of obstacles and dangers.
PRINCESS F.	I can overcome them all, Father. I want to fulfill a great task.
QUEEN F.	But how will you go such a long way alone?
PRINCESS F.	I can go with my horse, Benny, Mother. You know, there's a strong friendship between us. He understands me, and I understand him.
QUEEN F.	Of course, it's helpful that you know animal language. But still, we will be anxious about you.
PRINCESS F.	Please, Mother... Please, Father, trust me! Up to now, I have never crossed the borders of our Land of Flowers. I have not seen anywhere else. I do not know anyone except those living in this palace. I want to see new places and meet new people. Please let me go!

They freeze while the discussion continues.

1st PLAYER	After a long discussion...
2nd PLAYER	Princess Flower manages to persuade her parents.

KING F.	Alright my dear, you can go.
QUEEN F.	You can go, then.

Princess Flower kisses her parents and shouts joyously. They walk to the back of the stage.

PRINCESS F.	Hurray! I'll manage it, Father. I'll go and bring back flower seeds. I'll end our country's unfulfilled yearning for flowers.
2nd PLAYER	They started the preparations for the trip enthusiastically.
1st PLAYER	Finally, the time for the trip to begin was at hand.
2nd PLAYER	Princess Flower and Benny the horse got up early that morning.

The 1st PLAYER and the 2nd PLAYER wear their guards' helmets. They cross their lances in front of the gate of the palace. There is a basket on the arm of Princess Flower, and saddlebags and jugs on Benny's back. The Queen and the King are excited. Begonia looks at them from backstage.

BENNY	Why are we still waiting, Princess Flower?
PRINCESS F.	Don't be impatient, Benny. We'll set off in a minute.
BENNY	We had better set off now. Otherwise I'll burst into tears because I have to leave Begonia.
PRINCESS F.	(*Looks at Begonia*) We could have taken Begonia with us, but you know that we have an important

QUEEN F.	task. (*Gives her the basket she has prepared*) Are you ready, my daughter?
PRINCESS F.	Yes, Mother, we're ready. We're impatient to take to the road.
KING F.	You'll be ready as soon as you listen to our advice, my little daughter.
QUEEN F.	Listen to us very carefully, and don't forget what we say.
PRINCESS F.	I won't forget, Mother.
KING F.	You'll meet many obstacles on the way to the Land of Giants. You'll overcome them all, thanks to your wisdom, intelligence and personality. Never abandon goodwill towards others.
PRINCESS F.	OK, Father!
QUEEN F.	Always be polite and gentle. Help those who are in need.
PRINCESS F.	Don't worry about it, Mother!
BENNY	(*Neighs*) Come on, Princess Flower, we're late.
PRINCESS F.	Be a little patient, Benny. We'll leave soon.
KING F.	Always be generous, my daughter, don't be selfish. Don't forget that you can't be happy alone. Pains

	decrease as you share them, happiness increases as you share it. Never forget this.
PRINCESS F.	I'll never forget it, Father... Because you've always taught me this.
QUEEN F.	We trust you, our dear daughter. Always be fair and just. Being just is one of the greatest virtues of human beings. Always struggle against injustice. Defend those who are right, even if they are weak.
PRINCESS F.	I promise you, Mother. I'll always struggle against injustice and defend those who are right.
KING F.	Never forget what we've said to you now. Keep these things always in your mind.
PRINCESS F.	Don't worry, Father. I'll be a daughter who deserves your confidence.
KING F.	There are three big obstacles on the way to the Land of Giants. You'll first pass through the Great Forest and then the Red Desert. Next, you'll see the Lofty Mountain. You'll reach the Land of Giants once you pass over this mountain.
PRINCESS F.	I'll do my best to overcome all these obstacles.

QUEEN F.	My dear Princess. Please watch out for dangers and evils.
PRINCESS F.	I promise you, Mother. I'll take care of myself. I'll overcome all the obstacles. And I will bring back flower seeds to my Land of Flowers. I promise you.
BENNY	(*Grumbles, bucking.*) Hurry up, Princess Lily. We're late.
PRINCESS F.	(*To Benny*) Alright, Benny, Alright. I'm coming. Goodbye, Mother.

They hug each other.

QUEEN F.	(*Kisses her daughter*) Goodbye my daughter. Take care.
PRINCESS F.	Goodbye, Father.

They hug each other.

KING F.	Take good care of yourself. We'll be looking forward to your safe return.
BENNY	(*Neighs*) Goodbye, my Begonia. I look forward to leaving now and coming back to you as soon as possible.
BEGONIA	(*Neighs*) Goodbye, my Benny. I'll be waiting for you impatiently

Princess Flower mounts Benny. They set off. The guards uncross their lances. Princess Flower, who rides on Benny, passes between the guards. Princess Flower and Benny look back. Princess Flower and those watching wave to each other. Benny and Begonia neigh dolefully. They freeze. The 1st PLAYER and the 2nd PLAYER revert to their original roles.

A PLEASANT JOURNEY

Princess Flower, who rides on her horse Benny, circles the stage a few times while the narrators explain to the audience what is happening.

2nd PLAYER	They moved away from the palace of the Land of Flowers...
1st PLAYER	They crossed the borders of the Land of Flowers...
2nd PLAYER	They rode and rode...
1st PLAYER	They passed over mountains and plains...
2nd PLAYER	They became tired and stopped to rest...
1st PLAYER	Then they set off again.
2nd PLAYER	They became hungry and thirsty...
1st PLAYER	But they didn't mind and went on.
PRINCESS F.	How wonderful it is to see new places.
BENNY	How about the long roads and the tiredness we feel as we pass these new places?
PRINCESS F.	Are you very tired, my dear Benny?
BENNY	Yes, really tired. I already miss our Land of Flowers.
PRINCESS F.	Don't say that, Benny. We'd better go back, if you say such things.

BENNY	No, my Princess Flower. I'm tired but we can't go back. I'll get rid of my tiredness after we take a rest somewhere.
PRINCESS F.	Then let me dismount. Let's walk together. I can't ride on you when you're tired.
BENNY	Thank you, Princess Flower. How kind-hearted you are.

Princess Flower dismounts and they continue circling the stage together.

PRINCESS F.	We are getting close to the Great Forest.
BENNY	I smell fresh grass and leaves.
PRINCESS F.	I hope there's water, too. If only I could wash my hands and face, and cool off a little bit.

They freeze.

FIRST OBSTACLE – THE GREAT FOREST

2nd PLAYER	In the end they reached the Great Forest.
1st PLAYER	They were very happy when they reached the Great Forest.

Princess Flower and Benny circle the stage once more. The PLAYERS, holding tree branches which resemble trees, come from the opposite side and walk in the reverse direction. Then they come across Princess Flower and Benny again. Hence, the illusion that Princess Flower and Benny walk through the forest is displayed theatrically. Moreover, the PLAYERS create the atmosphere of a great forest with sounds and various objects. Each PLAYER is a tree.

PRINCESS F.	This is a wonderful forest. Wonderful.
BENNY	Let's see whether it has wonderful grass.
PRINCESS F.	How cool it is. How deep the shadows of the trees are. Look, do you know the names of these trees?
BENNY	That is as easy as falling off a log. That one is a pine tree. This is a plane. Those are acacias. These are poplars. And the one behind them is a juniper. Look, those are willows. I don't like to eat

PRINCESS F.	the leaves of any of them except for willow leaves. (*Takes a deep breath*) How fresh the air is here.
BENNY	Let's find a comfortable green area. Let me take a breath. I feel as if I'm going to fall down here and now, I'm so tired.

One of the PLAYERS makes them meet a male and a female nightingale, represented by hand puppets.

FEMALE NIGHTINGALE	Hello. I'm the female nightingale of this forest.
MALE NIGHTINGALE	And I'm the male nightingale of this forest. Hello.
PRINCESS F.	Hello, dear nightingales. My name is Lily. And this is my friend, Benny.
BENNY	Hello.
MALE NIGHTINGALE	Welcome to our forest.
FEMALE NIGHTINGALE	Welcome to our forest.
PRINCESS F.	Thank you, lovely nightingales. How hospitable you are. And how lovely your songs are.
MALE NIGHTINGALE	Thank you.
FEMALE NIGHTINGALE	Can we sing for you?

BENNY	(*Grumbles*) No, thanks.
PRINCESS F.	We'll be very pleased.
FEMALE NIGHTINGALE	Alright then, we will begin...
MALE NIGHTINGALE	We will begin then.
FEMALE NIGHTINGALE	We sing our songs day and night...
MALE NIGHTINGALE	This is our delight.
FEMALE NIGHTINGALE	We cheer up the forest...
MALE NIGHTINGALE	With our lovely songs.
PRINCESS F.	Thank you very much. How marvellous your song is!
FEMALE NIGHTINGALE	Thank you...
MALE NIGHTINGALE	Thank you.

The nightingales go on singing, hopping from one branch to another, without moving away from Princess Flower and Benny.

PRINCESS F.	The sound the nightingales make is very beautiful, isn't it?
BENNY	(*Grumbles*) Yes, not bad.
PRINCESS F.	Don't be jealous, Benny. The sound they make is really very good.
BENNY	Alright, alright, it's fine.

They continue walking on the stage, as if they were passing through the forest. Two PLAYERS characterize deer, one of which has fallen into a trap.

PRINCESS F.	Oh, look, Benny, do you see that?
BENNY	(*Indifferently*) I see two deer.
PRINCESS F.	Oh, Benny, how indifferent you are!
BENNY	But why?
PRINCESS F.	Look, they don't seem well. Let's go to them.
BENNY	Let's go and see.

Walking more rapidly, they go up to the deer. The buck has fallen into a trap made of netted rope. The hind waits besides him unhappily.

PRINCESS F.	What happened to you dearest deer?
HIND	We're desperate. We were grazing. I need to produce more milk for our fawns.
BUCK	Suddenly this net fell on me. I can't get rid of it, whatever I do.
HIND	I can't leave him. But I can't do anything to help him, either. I can't rescue my spouse from this trap.
BUCK	We don't know what to do now. We're waiting here in fear of hunters.

HIND	Our fawns are waiting for us. Please help us.
PRINCESS F.	Come on, Benny. Let's help and rescue the dear buck from this trap.
BENNY	Us? How can we rescue him?
PRINCESS F.	You can gnaw the net with your teeth.
BENNY	I'd rather eat fresh grass.
HIND	Please help us.
BUCK	We'll never forget to do you a favour sometime, if you help us.
BENNY	What favour can a deer do for me?
PRINCESS F.	Don't be so selfish, Benny. We have to help animals and human beings in need. Come on, please, start to gnaw the net.
HIND	Please. It'll be too late if the hunters come.
BENNY	Alright, alright. I'm trying. I hope the ropes won't set my teeth on edge. (*Benny starts to gnaw the rope.*) Oh, this rope is very thick and hard. And it smells very bad.
PRINCESS F.	Come on, Benny, courage! Let's rescue the dear buck. His fawns are waiting for him at home.

BENNY	Alright, alright. I'm gnawing.

Princess Flower and the Hind encourage him.

PRINCESS F.	Hurry up, Benny, there are only a few knots left.
HIND	You gnaw the net very well, friend Benny.
BENNY	The knots are endless.
PRINCESS F.	There are only a few left, only a few. Please be patient.

In the end the deer is completely freed from the net.

BENNY	I've finished it.
BUCK	(*Rescued*) Oh, at last I'm free. Long live freedom!
HIND	Thank God! Thank you very much, both of you.
BUCK	Thank you very much.
BENNY	(*Boastfully*) Not at all. It was a piece of cake for me.
PRINCESS F.	Well done, dear Benny! That was a difficult task you managed.
HIND	At last we can see our fawns again. We'll never forget the favour you've done us.
BUCK	We want to return the favour sometime.
PRINCESS F.	But we're not expecting compensation for what we've done, are we, Benny?

BENNY	(*Grumbles*) No, no.
HIND	It seems that you have a long way to go. You may get hungry during your journey. I'd like to offer you my milk. Please milk me and get however much milk you want.
BENNY	(*Talks to himself*) I'd rather have an armful of clover.
PRINCESS F.	But your fawns need to drink your milk.
HIND	I have enough milk for them and you. Please milk me and get some milk. I'll be pleased if you do. My milk helps many illnesses, you know.
BUCK	My spouse is very generous. She'll be pleased to give you her milk.
HIND	Please do! My milk is clean, healthy and nutritious, you know.
BENNY	Come on, Princess Flower, milk her and let's go. Otherwise I'll begin to eat bark because I'm so hungry.
PRINCESS F.	Alright then. Let me milk into a milk-jug.

Princess Flower milks from the udders of the deer into the jug. The other PLAYERS create the effect of milking.

PRINCESS F.	This is fine. This is enough for me. I mustn't take all your milk. Thank you very much, dear hind.
HIND	I hope it will help you. It'll provide you with good health.
PRINCESS F.	We'd better set off, hadn't we dear Benny?
BENNY	Let's find a fountain. Otherwise I'll die of thirst.
HIND	We know a nice fountain close at hand.
BUCK	There are fresh grasses and huge trees around it. We can show it to you.
BENNY	Excellent. It sounds great.
PRINCESS F.	But your fawns are waiting for you. You shouldn't be late.
BUCK	No, we won't be late. It's on the way home.
PRINCESS F.	Then let's go without dawdling.
BENNY	Hurray, at last we'll have water to drink.

They circle the stage for some time. The deer lead, and Princess Flower and Benny follow them. Then they freeze.

1st PLAYER	Following the deer, Princess Flower and Benny the horse walked through the depths of

	the Great Forest
2nd PLAYER	They walked under huge trees...
1st PLAYER	They walked over flowers and grasses...
2nd PLAYER	They walked beside birds and insects...
1st PLAYER	And in the end they reached the fountain.
2nd PLAYER	Wishing them good luck, the deer left them to return home.

The PLAYERS acting the deer revert to their original roles and remove the deer accessories. At the same time the 1st PLAYER and the 2nd PLAYER create a huge tree with the help of props. They make nests on the trees with some pieces of cloth and place puppets representing eagle fledglings in them. They create a fountain, making use of various other props, and they represent the water of the fountain with a piece of blue cloth.

PRINCESS F.	This place is wonderful, Benny, isn't it?
BENNY	Yes, wonderful. And that grass looks great.
PRINCESS F.	Let's try the water of this lovely fountain! (*Goes up to the "fountain", cups her hands to catch the water, and drinks from them, several times. She washes her hands and face.*) Oh, great! I have cooled off.

BENNY	*(Drinks the water deeply)*
PRINCESS F.	We can eat something here and catch our breath.
BENNY	How well you speak, Princess Flower. You talk about the matters that I love most.
FEMALE NIGHTINGALE	*(Comes near them, singing)* Are you stopping here?
PRINCESS F.	Yes, it's very lovely here.
MALE NIGHTINGALE	We can sing for you whenever you want.
BENNY	*(Grumbles to himself)* No, thanks.
PRINCESS F.	Thank you very much, dear nightingales.

The nightingales begin to sing. Princess Flower sits on the ground. She spreads a cloth and prepares something for herself to eat. Benny mimes eating grass.

BENNY	Hmmm, the grass of this forest is very delicious. Excellent.
PRINCESS F.	I'm impatient to drink the deer's milk. I have missed the taste of milk.

A PLAYER in the costume of a snake approaches the tree, crawling and hissing. The fledglings in the nest begin to chirp.

PRINCESS F.	What's happening? Why are these birds chirping?

MALE NIGHTINGALE	(*Anxiously*) This is the Grand Snake. It's crawling up the trunk of the tree and along a branch.
PRINCESS F.	Is it crawling up the trunk of the tree and along a branch?
FEMALE NIGHTINGALE	Yes, it's going to the nest of the white eagles...
MALE NIGHTINGALE	It's going to eat their fledglings.
BENNY	But that's criminal.
PRINCESS F.	How about their mother and father?
MALE NIGHTINGALE	They aren't here. They've gone to find something for their fledglings to eat.

In the meantime, the Grand Snake crawls up and along the tree created by the PLAYERS.

PRINCESS F.	We have to do something. We have to prevent it.
BENNY	But how?! I can't kick it there, up on the tree.
FEMALE NIGHTINGALE	We're not strong enough to resist it.
PRINCESS F.	Maybe we can find a more peaceful way. (*Calls the snake*) Grand Snake! Grand Snake! Don't harm the fledglings!
SNAKE	It's easy for you to say that. Am I to die of hunger?!

PRINCESS F.	But they're so small. You can't be so pitiless?!
SNAKE	You're right, they are small. But I haven't eaten anything since morning.
FEMALE NIGHTINGALE	Listen to them screaming!
MALE NIGHTINGALE	Don't you feel pity for them?
SNAKE	Look, don't annoy me or I shall eat you too.
MALE NIGHTINGALE	It's not that easy. Do you think we would alight near you?
FEMALE NIGHTINGALE	You can only attack vulnerable fledglings in their nest.
BENNY	I'm hungry too, but I don't attempt to eat anyone.
PRINCESS F.	(*Adopting a conciliatory attitude*) Look, Grand Snake, I understand that you're hungry. But you don't have the right to eat those little birds. Let's make an agreement.
SNAKE:	(*Seems interested*) What kind of an agreement?
BENNY	(*In a low voice*) I also wonder what Princess Flower has in mind.
PRINCESS F.	We'll give you something to

	eat and in return you won't harm the fledglings.
BENNY	(*To the snake*) Not a bad idea. Why don't you think about it.
SNAKE	I'll think about it if you offer me something good.
PRINCESS F.	As far as I know, snakes like milk a lot.
SNAKE	Is there milk here? Are you offering me milk?
BENNY	(*To Princess Flower*) Will you really give your milk to that snake?
PRINCESS F.	Yes, I would like to drink it myself, but it's more important to save the fledglings.
MALE NIGHTINGALE	You'd better not miss this chance.
BENNY	How about you, what will you eat?
PRINCESS F.	I haven't thought about that. I'm sure I can find something to eat. At the moment, it's vital to save the fledglings.
SNAKE:	(*Hastily*) Alright. I accept your offer.
FEMALE NIGHTINGALE	Hurray, the fledglings will be saved!
PRINCESS F.	Thank you very much, Grand Snake. I will leave the milk-

SNAKE	jug here. You can drink from it whenever you want. It's been a long time since I last drank milk.

Princess Flower leaves the milk-jug. The snake crawls up to it and mimes drinking the milk.

FEMALE NIGHTINGALE	Hurray! The fledglings are saved.
MALE NIGHTINGALE	Mother White Eagle and Father White Eagle will be very happy. (*They continue hopping from one branch to another, singing. Princess Flower and Benny freeze.*)
1st PLAYER	Princess Flower and Benny the horse slept well in the forest that night.
2nd PLAYER	The water of the fountain was like a lullaby for them both.
1st PLAYER	They got up early next morning...
2nd PLAYER	To overcome the second obstacle...
1st PLAYER	To pass through the Red Desert...
2nd PLAYER	They set off.

SECOND OBSTACLE – THE RED DESERT

Princess Flower and Benny set off. They circle the entire stage.

2nd PLAYER	Walking and resting...
1st PLAYER	Crying and laughing...
2nd PLAYER	Wondering and puzzling...
1st PLAYER	They moved away from the Great Forest...
2nd PLAYER	And reached the Red Desert.

Benny takes a new position in the desert as if walking on a path. Princess Flower is riding on him. They continue circling the stage. The other PLAYERS make them encounter rocks, cactuses, sand-hills, and suchlike, around the stage, making use of miscellaneous props.

BENNY	(*Sweating*) Ouff. It's very hot.
PRINCESS F.	Don't say that, Benny. You're an experienced horse. Don't give up.
BENNY	Is it easy to resist this hot sun? (*Reproachfully*) Especially when there's such a load on me.
PRINCESS F.	(*Smiles*) Alright. I will dismount. I'll walk with you.

Dismounts and begins to walk with Benny.

PRINCESS F.	You have to bear it. We have to overcome this obstacle.
BENNY	I'm not a camel. How shall I bear this heat? What if we go back?

PRINCESS F.	It isn't possible, Benny. We have to reach the Land of Giants and get flower seeds.
BENNY	Yes. But if only there were some shade over us.
PRINCESS F.	If only we'd brought a few branches along with us.
BENNY	If only...! They would shade us. How hot the sun is.
PRINCESS F.	You're right. But we have no choice. We have to pass through this desert
BENNY	Ouff. We'll turn into vapour if it goes on like this.
PRINCESS F.	Resist, Benny. We can manage it. We have to resist.
BENNY	It's easy for you to say. Ouff. Ouff.

The PLAYERS make two big White Eagle puppets fly side by side in the sky, manipulating them with long sticks and ropes. Their shadow falls on Princess Flower and Benny.

BENNY	(*Startled*) What's that?
PRINCESS F.	(*Raising her head and looking up*) Oh look, two white eagles!
BENNY	(*Anxious*) I hope they won't harm us. My father told me that desert eagles were very dangerous.
PRINCESS F.	They don't look like dangerous eagles.
BENNY	Their shadow is very comforting. But what if they harm us?!

PRINCESS F	Don't worry, Benny. Let's ask them what they want.
BENNY	Isn't it clear? They're going to plunge down on us with their sharp beaks whenever they get a chance.
PRINCESS F.	(*Raising her head, shouts at the puppets representing eagles*) White Eagles! White Eagles! What do you want from us? Why are you flying over us?
M. EAGLE	Don't be afraid! Don't be afraid of us! We're your friends.
F. EAGLE	We're your friends, don't be afraid of us. We'd like to thank you.
PRINCESS F.	(*Surprised, joyful*) Did you hear them, Benny?
F. EAGLE	We heard that you saved our fledglings from the Grand Snake.
M. EAGLE	We're following you to thank you.
BENNY	(*Joyfully*) I'm happy to hear it.
F. EAGLE	Thank you.
PRINCESS F.	Not at all. We felt pity for your little fledglings. We just wanted to protect them. Anyone would have done the same thing.
BENNY	(*In a low voice*) I'm not sure about it. I don't know if anybody else would have given milk to the snake.

M. EAGLE	We'd like to do you a favour.
F. EAGLE	Ask us whatever you wish.
PRINCESS F.	(*To Benny*) I don't know what to say. (*Looking up*) We didn't help your fledglings, expecting a reward. Thank you very much. We don't need anything.
BENNY	But it'll be fine if they go on casting a shadow over us.
M. EAGLE	Please, tell us what you want...
F. EAGLE	Tell us what you want, please.
PRINCESS F.	Alright then. We have just one wish. My horse and I would be very pleased if you would go on providing shade for us until we pass through this desert.
F. EAGLE	We'll be pleased to accompany you. We'll be happy.
M. EAGLE	Our shadow will be on you whenever you want...
F.EAGLE	The direct sunlight won't fall on you.
PRINCESS F.	Thank you very much.
BENNY	Hurray. We'll walk in shade.
PRINCESS F.	Look, Benny, the desert seems more beautiful now. (*Finds stones on the ground*) Look, Benny, look, stones of the desert. How beautiful they are.

They come across one of the female PLAYERS in the costume of a rabbit. This female rabbit is walking with difficulty under the hot sun.

PRINCESS F.	Oh, look Benny, what a lovely rabbit!
BENNY	Look how she's sweating. (*Laughs*) She must have sunstroke. She's swaying from side to side.
PRINCESS F.	Don't be rude, Benny. You were doing the same thing a short while ago.
BENNY	(*Laughs, neighing*) Hey, Rabbit! Rabbit! Are you having fun in the sun?
PRINCESS F.	You're not polite at all, Benny.
RABBIT	(*Sniffling*) No, I am not having fun. I'm sweltering in the sun. Besides, I'm afraid that those eagles will harm me. What will my children and my spouse do if the eagles harm me?
PRINCESS F.	Don't worry, lovely Rabbit. They're kind-hearted eagles. And they're our friends.
RABBIT	Oh, how benevolent your friends are. If only I had such benevolent friends to protect me.
BENNY	(*Boastfully*) But it's not that easy to gain friends. If you do a favour for someone, he can be your friend.
PRINCESS F.	(*To Benny*) I'm pleased that you came to this conclusion, dear

	Benny. (*To the rabbit*) Dear Rabbit, maybe the white eagles may allow you to make use of their shadow. Let's ask them.
RABBIT	That would be great. Otherwise, I'm afraid I'll die in this desert without reaching my home.
PRINCESS F.	(*Calls the white eagles*) Dear White Eagles!
M. EAGLE	What's the problem, Princess Flower, what do you want?
F. EAGLE	Isn't our shadow enough?
PRINCESS F.	No, dear White Eagles, we're pleased with the shade your shadow gives us.
BENNY	We're very pleased.
PRINCESS F.	But we have met a new friend. A lovely rabbit. Can she also make use of your shadow?
F. EAGLE	Of course, she can. You needn't have asked.
M. EAGLE	Our shadow is yours. Everyone that you want can make use of it. We'll be pleased.
RABBIT	Hurray.
PRINCESS F.	Thank you very much, dear White Eagles. (*To the rabbit*) Come under the shadow, dear Rabbit.
RABBIT	This is so generous. Thank you very much.
PRINCESS F.	(*To Benny*) I think that you should carry her on your back to allow

	her to rest for a little bit.
BENNY	Who? Me?
PRINCESS F.	Wasn't it you who said that you had to help someone to gain his friendship?
BENNY	But. But I said it for the rabbit.
PRINCESS F.	Yes, but the rabbit is in need now.
RABBIT	Please, don't argue because of me. It's enough for me to have this shade. I'll try to keep up with you, though I'm tired.
PRINCESS F.	Come on, Benny.
BENNY	Alright, but what will she do for me?
PRINCESS F.	We don't do favours expecting a reward, Benny. You mustn't think like that.
BENNY	Alright, alright, she can ride on me.
PRINCESS F.	Yes, you're really a "Horse Flower now". (*To the rabbit*) Come on, dear Rabbit. (*She helps the rabbit get on Benny.*) You can take a rest here thanks to Benny.
RABBIT	Thank you very much. Thank you very much, dear Benny. I'll never forget your friendship.
BENNY	(*Grumbles*) Not at all… I hope you won't forget.
PRINCESS F.	Dear Rabbit, where do you come from, where are you going? What are you doing here, in this Red

RABBIT	Desert? I was leading a happy life with my spouse and leverets on the Lofty Mountain.
PRINCESS F.	So, why are you in this desert?
RABBIT	The desert lion attacked our home. My spouse and I tried to defend our leverets. The lion caught and kidnapped me while I was trying to protect my young ones. And the lion took me to its home in this desert.
BENNY	Hmm. What a pity! How were you rescued?
RABBIT	I escaped secretly while the lion was preparing to eat me.
PRINCESS F.	Thank God that you're safe now. We're also going to the Lofty Mountain. We can go together...
BENNY	But not all the way on my back.
RABBIT	Don't worry, dear Benny. I'll dismount and walk with you as soon as I have rested a little.

They freeze.

1st PLAYER	Princess Flower and Benny pass through the desert, talking to their new friend, Rabbit.

The PLAYERS *begin to form a symbolic mountain, making use of the platforms on the stage.*

RABBIT	(*Jumping with joy*) Hurray! Finally we have arrived at my

BENNY	homeland. Thank you so much. Not at all. I'm happy I've gained a lovely new friend.
PRINCESS F.	We have to thank the white eagles.
RABBIT	You're right. (*Looks up*) Thank you very much, dear White Eagles...
PRINCESS F.	Thank you very much for casting your shadow over us...
BENNY	Thank you very much for protecting us from the sun.
F. EAGLE	Not at all, dear friends.
M. EAGLE	It was a great pleasure for us to help you.
F. EAGLE	So now we're going back. Dear friends...
M. EAGLE	We'll come and help you with pleasure whenever you call us...
F. EAGLE	Just call our names three times in succession.
PRINCESS F.	How kind-hearted you are. Thank you very much.
M. EAGLE	We wish you a good journey.
F. EAGLE	Goodbye...
M. EAGLE	Goodbye...
EVERYONE	Goodbye. Thank you very much.
RABBIT	Now it's time for me to help you. I'm going to guide you over the Lofty Mountain and show you all the paths.
PRINCESS F.	You're very kind-hearted, dear

Rabbit. We need your help very much.

They freeze. After flying in the reverse direction for some time, the Eagles go out of sight. The PLAYERS playing the role of the eagles join the other PLAYERS.

THE THIRD OBSTACLE
THE LOFTY MOUNTAIN

The PLAYERS create ascending and descending mountain paths, making use of various accessories.

1st PLAYER	The three friends begin to climb the Lofty Mountain...
2nd PLAYER	They take a rest when they get tired...
1st PLAYER	They go on climbing up after each rest...
1st PLAYER	They get hungry, they get thirsty...
2nd PLAYER	With the help of the rabbit, they find fresh grass and other herbs to eat. They eat these heartily...
1st PLAYER	They quaff the water of cold springs.

The effect of a breeze is created, using various objects.

PRINCESS F.	How steadily it blows. It cools us off.
RABBIT	It's alright here, but the wind blows more harshly in higher parts. It sometimes turns into a storm.
BENNY	Really? I hate harsh winds.
PRINCESS F.	Look at those gorgeous grasses. Each and every one is different and more beautiful than the others.
RABBIT	I like them very much.

PRINCESS F.   How about these flowers ? You can't find some of them even in our Land of Flowers.

All of a sudden, the PLAYERS and musicians create the effects of howling.

BENNY   (*Stops fearfully*) What's that?
RABBIT   The howling of wolves. Let's not go in that direction. Let's go in this direction instead. Then, we can escape from the wolves.
BENNY   Really?
RABBIT   We won't come across them if we take this path. I know these ways very well.
PRINCESS F.   Thank you very much, dear Rabbit. You are saving us from all the dangers of the mountain.
BENNY   Ohhh, I'm very afraid of wolves. And I'm very tired. (*Grouses*) How will we pass over this huge Lofty Mountain?
PRINCESS F.   We have to endure, my dear Benny.
BENNY   But I'm very tired. We've been walking for days. I can't bear it any more. We'd better go back to our home.
PRINCESS F.   We'd better go back? You know that's not possible, Benny, my dear horse. It's not possible after we have come so far.

BENNY	But I don't have the power to take even one more step. Look how high the Lofty Mountain is. How can we pass over it? We don't have the strength to pass over it. You don't know how much I miss our Land of Flowers and my Begonia. We'd better go back before we run into trouble.
PRINCESS F.	But Benny, my dear horse, our citizens in the Land of Flowers are expecting us to bring back flower seeds. They can't grow flowers if we don't take them any seeds. Our country may remain a wasteland. Do we have the right to disappoint our Flower Citizens?
BENNY	Tell them to get the flower seeds themselves if it's that easy.
PRINCESS F.	They could have come, but we undertook this task. We have to complete the task we have undertaken. Otherwise how will we face them again?
BENNY	(*Sad*) You're right, Princess Flower. But it seems very difficult to go on. How will we pass over the Lofty Mountain?
PRINCESS F.	We can do it. We passed the Great Forest and the Red Desert. And we can pass over the Lofty Mountain, too.

RABBIT	There's no need to be afraid of the Lofty Mountain, dear friends. The Lofty Mountain is high, but it doesn't obstruct those who strive to pass over it. Besides, I'll help you.
PRINCESS F.	Thank you very much, dear Rabbit. Haven't we reached your home yet?
RABBIT	We have passed it, but I'll guide you to the borders of the Land of Giants. Then I'll return home.
PRINCESS F.	You're very self-sacrificing, dear Rabbit... Thank you very much.
RABBIT	Not at all... We're friends, aren't we?
PRINCESS F.	Your companionship is a piece of good luck for us. We'd better keep going without wasting time, hadn't we, dear Benny?
BENNY	(*Reluctantly*) Alright, let's go on.

They start to walk again. They freeze.

1st PLAYER	They began to climb up to the summit of the mountain with difficulty.
2nd PLAYER	The path became more and more demanding as they climbed, and the slope became steeper.
1st PLAYER	It was colder. And the wind was harsher.

Princess Flower, Benny and the rabbit move again. With the help of other PLAYERS and the musicians, the 1st PLAYER and the 2nd PLAYER create the effects of thunder, lightning, and wind, making use of objects such as sheet metal.

RABBIT	Hey! Let's take this path, not that one. This is a shortcut. The other path is full of rocks.
BENNY	O..h..h, I don't like rocks on paths at all. Let's not go that way. It's getting rather cold. Even I feel cold.
PRINCESS F.	The clouds have completely covered the sun.
RABBIT	Yes, black clouds.
BENNY	I have the impression that it'll start raining soon.

The rain effects begin.

RABBIT	It has already started. The rain drops are wetting my ears.
PRINCESS F.	It has really started to rain.
BENNY	I think we'll die on this mountain and be the dinner of wolves.

The PLAYERS reinforce the effect of rain.

PRINCESS	It's pouring down more heavily.
BENNY	We're ruined.
RABBIT	There must be a cave somewhere here.
PRINCESS F.	Really?

BENNY	Please, dear friend Rabbit, find a solution.
RABBIT	Is it in this direction? No, no, in that direction.
BENNY	Alas. I'll look like a drowned rat soon.
RABBIT	Oh, yes, I remember. Over there. We'll reach it when we pass that small hill. Let's walk faster...
PRINCESS F.	Alright, let's walk faster...
BENNY	I can even run to reach the cave.

They circle the stage rapidly. The PLAYERS create a hole from rocks. They shelter in the hole.

BENNY	Hurray, we're saved. I won't go any further until the rain stops.
PRINCESS F.	What luck you found this little cave for us. Otherwise we would have been ruined.
RABBIT	I'm sorry. I haven't been to this part of the mountain for a long time. I couldn't easily remember where the cave was.

They freeze.

1st PLAYER	They took a much-needed rest in the cave.
2nd PLAYER	When the rain stopped, the sun rose and it warmed everything.
2nd PLAYER	They set off again.

They are on the way. They are going downhill. They are

joyful.

BENNY — Hurray! The rain clouds have disappeared.
PRINCESS F. — How lovely the warm sun is!
RABBIT — Yes, great! I love snow but the sun isn't bad, either.
BENNY — It's easier to go downhill.
RABBIT — It's harder for me because my front legs are shorter. But it doesn't matter. I don't mind anything now we have survived the storm.

They walk further.

RABBIT — Here is the Land of Giants. I hope you will manage to get in through the palace gate.
PRINCESS F. — We have passed over the Lofty Mountain thanks to you. We're now closer to our objective.
BENNY — Thank you, friend Rabbit. It was a good piece of luck that we came across you in the desert.
RABBIT — I'm very pleased also to have met you. Otherwise I couldn't have passed through the desert and reached home.
PRINCESS F. — Go now, don't worry your family any longer.
RABBIT — Yes, I'd like to go back to my spouse and children if you're

PRINCESS F.	willing for me to go now. You'll be late, dear Rabbit. Thank you very much for guiding us to the Land of Giants.
RABBIT	It's enough to call my name three times whenever you need me. I'll hear you wherever I am and come to help you. Goodbye.
PRINCESS F.	Goodbye, dear Rabbit… We'll never forget you…
BENNY	Goodbye, my dear friend, Rabbit.

They freeze as Rabbit leaves.

1st PLAYER	Princess Flower turns her horse out to graze.
2nd PLAYER	She approaches the palace of the Land of Giants alone.
1st PLAYER	What do you think she saw when she reached the gate of the palace?

THE PALACE OF THE LAND OF GIANTS

There is a Watch Horse and a Watch Dog in front of the gate of the palace. There is a ham in front of the Horse and a bale of hay in front of the Dog. Their leashes are very short. The Horse smells the ham in front of it and stamps its feet, whereas the Dog smells the hay in front of it and barks furiously. Princess Flower tries to get closer to them but she cannot. She seems bewildered.

DOG	(*Barking*) You can't enter. Bow wow. Bow wow. You can't enter. Bow wow.
HORSE	(*Neighing*) You can't pass over, hiiiii. You can't pass over. hiiiiiiii.
PRINCESS F.	Dear Horse! Dear Dog! Please be calm! Please! What are you doing here? What's happening?
HORSE	I'm hungry. I've been hungry for days...
DOG	I'm hungry. I've been hungry for months, for days.
PRINCESS F.	But there's plenty of ham and hay in front of you. Why don't you eat them?
HORSE	Because the hay is in front of him...
DOG	Because the ham is in front of him.
PRINCESS F.	But why? Why don't you change your food?
DOG	Because we're tied up...

HORSE	Because we're tied up.
PRINCESS F.	Who tied you up?
HORSE	The Queen of the Giants...
DOG	The Giant of the Queens.
PRINCESS F.	But why? Why did she tie you up here?
DOG	She punished us...
HORSE	The Queen punished us.
PRINCESS F.	She punished you? Why did she punish this lovely horse and this lovely dog? What did you do for her to punish you?
HORSE	I kicked the female horse while running...
DOG	I bit the female dog while playing.
PRINCESS F.	Oh, oh.
HORSE	And the Queen of Giants punished us.
DOG	She made us sentries at the Palace of Giants.
PRINCESS F.	What a pity.
DOG	She put a bale of hay in front of me and a ham in front of him.
HORSE	She left us hungry for days.
PRINCESS F.	Whew! Whew!
DOG	I'm barking because of hunger. I'm howling because of anger.
HORSE	I'm kicking because of anger. I'm neighing because of rage.
PRINCESS F.	But it's not good manners to kick or bite your spouses.

DOG	We know. We've understood it now.
HORSE	Now we've understood it. We know.
PRINCESS F.	But this is a very severe punishment.
HORSE	A very severe punishment. Very severe.
DOG	Very severe. A very severe punishment.
PRINCESS F.	I believe you. I believe that you're now aware of your mistake. That's why I take back your punishment.
HORSE	No, don't do that.
DOG	Don't do that.
HORSE	The Queen of Giants will punish you, too.
DOG	She may send you to a dungeon.
PRINCESS F.	I will take the risk. As my parents said, I should always defend those who are right. I don't do anything bad. I take responsibility for all my actions. (*She puts the ham in front of the Dog, and the hay in front of the Horse.*)
HORSE	Hurray.
DOG	You're great.
HORSE	(*Begins to eat the hay*) How kind-hearted you are.
DOG	(*Begins to eat the ham*) How

HORSE	kind-hearted you are. We're going to open the gates of the Palace for you.
DOG	We're going to let you enter the Palace of Giants.
PRINCESS F.	Thank you very much, but you can be punished again for this act.
HORSE	We will face the consequences.
DOG	Yes, we will face the consequences …

The Horse and the Dog step to one side to make way for Princess Flower. The Princess begins to open the gate of the Palace, and she freezes in that position. The other PLAYERS begin to create the King of Giants and the Queen of Giants. One PLAYER stands on the shoulders of another PLAYER and wearing a long costume performs the role of each character.

2nd PLAYER	The gates of the Palace of Giants were wide open in front of Princess Flower.
1st PLAYER	Princess Flower walked through huge halls and climbed up huge stairs.
2nd PLAYER	In the end she found herself in the presence of the King of Giants and the Queen of Giants.
1st PLAYER	She was afraid and excited at the same time.

The Queen of the Giants and the King of the Giants sit side by side on a throne. A giant female guard stands beside the

King, and a giant male guard stands beside the Queen. Princess Flower greets the King of the Giants and the Queen of the Giants in her own way. The body of the King and Queen are each formed by two PLAYERS, one standing on the other's shoulders. Whenever the player performing a head says something, the other player – unseen under the costume – repeats the words, creating an echo effect. The voice of the Queen is echoed by a male PLAYER, and the voice of the King is echoed by a female PLAYER.

GIANT KING	Who are you? What do you want? What are you doing here?
GIANT QUEEN	What are you doing here alone, you, a young girl?
PRINCESS F.	(*Afraid and excited*) My name is Princess Flower. I come from the Land of Flowers. I am the daughter of the King of the Land of Flowers. Why do you think that being a girl is a deficiency? Women are able to manage many things that men can do. I have overcome lots of obstacles to be here. I may be very young and inexperienced, but I'm not ignorant. Yes, experience is acquired through age, but knowledge can be gained at any age. Our ancestors say that wisdom isn't a product of age, but of knowledge. My parents made me what I am. I don't believe that I'm ignorant. I've

	come here to re-flower my Land of Flowers which has dried up. I came here to fetch seeds for my country.
GIANT QUEEN	Welcome, our beautiful guest, Princess Lily! We only played a joke on you...
GIANT KING	Our kind-hearted guest, Princess Lily, welcome! We only played a joke on you!
PRINCESS F.	(*Relieved*) Thank you very much! But... But how do you know me? How do you know my name?
GIANT QUEEN	We know everything...
GIANT KING	We know everyone.
GIANT QUEEN	We know why you came here...
GIANT KING	We know how you came here.
GIANT QUEEN	We know how you overcame all those obstacles...
GIANT KING	We know how kind-hearted you are...
GIANT QUEEN	We know how well-mannered you are.
PRINCESS F.	So you know that in front of the palace....
GIANT QUEEN	Yes, we know that...
GIANT KING	You put the hay in front of the Horse...

GIANT QUEEN	And the ham in front of the dog.
PRINCESS F.	I hope you're not angry with me for this.
GIANT QUEEN	No, no. On the contrary. On the contrary...
GIANT KING	We congratulate you for your courage.
PRINCESS F.	But...
GIANT QUEEN	I punished those animals because they mistreated their wives.
GIANT KING	It was a temporary punishment.
GIANT QUEEN	I would have cancelled their punishment when they became aware of their mistake.
PRINCESS F.	Are they aware of it?
GIANT KING	They are. They understood it very quickly.
PRINCESS F.	So?
GIANT QUEEN	We were waiting for a courageous person...
GIANT KING	A person who would cancel the punishment of the ham in front of the horse and the hay in front of the Dog...
GIANT QUEEN	And put the ham before the Horse before the Dog and the hay before the Dog before the Horse...
GIANT KING	You're that courageous person...
GIANT KING	We congratulate you for your courage, Princess Flower...

GIANT QUEEN	We congratulate you, Princess Flower.
PRINCESS F.	Thank you very much. So maybe you know the reason why the flowers in my Land of Flowers dried up.
GIANT QUEEN	Of course, we know it...
GIANT KING	We know it, of course.
PRINCESS F.	Why? Why did the flowers dry up?
G. QUEEN	Because women weren't allowed to work in the flower fields after your mother had fallen from the horse in the flower field.
GIANT KING	Women only work in their houses now...
GIANT QUEEN	Only men work in the flower fields now...
GIANT KING	That's why your flowers dried up.
PRINCESS F.	Really?
GIANT QUEEN	The flowers which aren't grown by men and women working together dry up...
GIANT KING	The meal which isn't made by men and women together is tasteless...
GIANT QUEEN	The children who aren't raised by men and women together are unhappy...
PRINCESS F.	Now I understand it. So you...?

GIANT KING	Yes, that's why we do everything together...
GIANT QUEEN	We rule the Land of Giants together...
GIANT KING	Men and women should do everything together...
GIANT QUEEN	They should sow the seeds together and grow the flowers together.
GIANT KING	The flowers will be more sturdy then...
GIANT QUEEN	Their flowers will gleam more...
GIANT KING	They'll smell better...
GIANT QUEEN	The honey made from these flowers will be more delicious.
GIANT KING	The citizens of such a country will be more powerful...
GIANT QUEEN	The children of such a country will be happier...
GIANT KING	The future of such a country will be brighter.
PRINCESS F.	Now I understand everything better. If only the unfulfilled yearning of our country for flowers would end. If only we could farm our lands all together as you said. We could be happy again.
GIANT QUEEN	The unfulfilled yearning of your country for flowers will end, Princess Flower.

GIANT KING	We'll give you the flower seeds you want.
PRINCESS F.	Hurray! Our citizens will be very happy.
GIANT QUEEN	But women should go to the flower fields with their men-folk from now on. They should grow the flowers together.
GIANT KING	Not only in the fields but also at home, at school, at work. Women and men should be together everywhere.
GIANT QUEEN	They should be equal, men and women, women and men. They should act hand in hand... Stand shoulder to shoulder...
GIANT KING	They should do everything together and share everything and anything.
PRINCESS F.	I'll tell all these ideas to my people, my mother, Queen Flower, and my father, King Flower. I'll do my best to ensure this equality in my country.
GIANT KING	This is what we expect from you, Princess Flower. You and all other young people are our hope...
GIANT QUEEN	Because you're the future of the Land of Flowers.
PRINCESS F.	Thank you very much. I promise you that I'll do my best.

GIANT QUEEN	We trust you, Princess Flower. (*Calls the guards*) Bring the flower seeds that Princess Flower wants.

Suddenly little colourful packets rain down. The guards do this. The packets are multicoloured. There are various flower pictures and motifs on the packets. Princess Flower begins to gather the packets joyously.

PRINCESS F.	Hurray! Flower seeds! Seeds of nice flowers! Hurray! My land will be covered with flowers again. My people will cheer up and be happy again. Children will be happy. Everything will be better again. Hurray.

Princess Flower freezes while appearing to gather up the packets of flower seeds.

A HAPPY RETURN HOME TO THE LAND OF FLOWERS

Princess Flower prepares Benny and loads the colourful packets of flower seeds onto his back. The Princess and Benny are on the way home. There are a few colourful packets of flower seeds in Princess Flower's hands.

1st PLAYER	Princess Flower and the horse Benny journeyed back home after they got the packets of flower seeds.
2nd PLAYER	Their animal friends kept them company on their way home.
1st PLAYER	They helped them devotedly...
2nd PLAYER	They accompanied them heartily...
1st PLAYER	Guided them...
2nd PLAYER	Found food for them...
1st PLAYER	Showed the fountains to them...
2nd PLAYER	Provided shade for them.
1st PLAYER	In the end they reached the Land of Flowers.

Queen Flower, King Flower, Prince Flower, Begonia, as well as all other citizens, meet Princess Flower and Benny in the Land of Flowers. There are drums, pipes, trumpets, and suchlike in their hands. In addition, the musical band can contribute to these festivities. There must be an atmosphere of joy and happiness on the stage. King Flower, Queen Flower and Prince Flower stand on a platform. The citizens take their places behind and beside them. The female horse, Begonia, tries to catch sight of Benny in the crowd.

EVERYONE	Long live Princess Flower! Long may she live! Long live Princess Flower! Long live Princess Flower!

The guards bring the packets of flower seeds to the platform where the King stands. Princess Flower hugs her mother first.

PRINCESS F.	Here I am, Mother. I managed it.
QUEEN F.	So you managed it and have come back. You can't imagine how proud and happy I am that I have a daughter like you!

Princess Flower hugs her father. Her father kisses her on the forehead.

KING F.	Welcome, my dear daughter.
PRINCESS F.	I'm not a boy but I managed it. I have brought back the flower seeds.
KING F.	I won't regret not having a son any more. I'm proud of you.
PRINCE F.	(*Hugs Princess Flower*) Welcome, my love.
PRINCESS F.	Thank you, darling.
PRINCE F.	So you managed it. We'll be able to sow and grow flowers again.
PRINCESS F.	Yes, we'll sow and grow flowers again. We'll again have flower harvest festivals.
PRINCE F.	So there's nothing to hinder our

	marriage. This is wonderful news.
PRINCESS F.	Yes, we'll get married in our flower country, now it is happy again.

Benny catches sight of Begonia. He neighs joyfully. Begonia neighs back joyfully. Prince Flower and Princess Flower kiss each other. The citizens applaud and cheer.

KING F.	(*Addresses the citizens*) My dear citizens... My daughter, Princess Lily, managed to reach the Land of Giants, overcoming all obstacles to bring back the flower seeds that our country needs. I congratulate her on behalf of you. Thank you, Princess Flower.
EVERYONE	Long live Princess Flower! May she live long! Thank you! May she live long! Long live Princess Flower! May she live long! Thank you! May she live long!
KING F.	I used to regret not having a son, a prince. However, my daughter has helped me overcome this regret. She has proved that women can do whatever men can do. I'm proud of her.
EVERYONE	Long live Princess Flower! May she live long! Thank you! May she live long! Long live Princess Flower! May she live long! Thank you! May she live long!...

PRINCESS F. (*Addressing the citizens*) My dear flower citizens, I'm happy that I could bring back flower seeds to our country. My horse Benny helped me a lot. I'd like to thank him.
EVERYONE Long live Benny the horse! May he live long! Long live Benny the horse! May he live long!

Benny neighs proudly and gratefully. Begonia flatters him with her neighs.

PRINCESS F. I bring you the love and greetings of the Queen of Giants and the King of Giants as well as the seeds. Also, I have learned why our flowers dried up.
EVERYONE (*Everyone is all ears*) Oh? Really? Why did our flowers dry up? What's the reason?
PRINCESS F. The reason is that our women didn't go into the fields. They didn't grow flowers with the men. Flowers need the hands of both men and women. Flowers which are not cared for by men and women together fade or dry up.
EVERYONE Oh? Really? So this was the reason? We understand it now. So that's why our flowers dried up? Hmmm. We understand it now!
KING F. My dear flower citizens! My

	distinguished flower citizens! I thought that I did women a favour when I forbade them to go to the flower fields to work. I thought that I was protecting them from danger. But now I understand that I harmed them and harmed our country through this decision. I apologize to our women and to you. I cancel this edict now.
EVERYONE	Long live our King Flower! Long live women! Long live women! Long live women!
KING F.	Now we're going to distribute the flower seeds that Princess Flower has brought us. We'll go to the fields together again, from now on. We'll sow and cultivate the flowers together again. Our harvest will become more fruitful and our harvest festival will become more joyful. Our Land of Flowers will blossom like a flower.
EVERYONE	Long live King Flower! Long live Princess Flower! Long live the Land of Flowers! Long live the Land of Flowers!

Princess Flower, Queen Flower, King Flower and Prince Flower pick up the little packets of flower seeds from the ground and throw them amongst the citizens. They say "Long live our flower citizens", "Long live our flower people" ,"Long live our land of flowers", while distributing the packets. The colourful packets of flower seeds create a colourful atmosphere on the stage. The citizens scramble to get the packets in childish joy. Then they freeze for a while.

THE WONDERFUL LAND OF FLOWERS ONCE MORE AND TOWARDS A MEANINGFUL END

1st PLAYER   The men and women of the Land of Flowers...
2nd PLAYER   began to grow flowers together.

The women and men of the Land of Flowers take their hoes and shovels. In a choreographed order, they act as if they are singing while working in the fields.

CITIZENS
Let us sow and scatter flower seeds
Using our hoes, shovels and hands;
Let us make everywhere flower
With our joy, love and songs.

The 1st PLAYER and the 2nd PLAYER hang flowers made of fabric or paper on rope at various spots on the stage to decorate it with flowers, to reinforce the image of the Land of Flowers. They can be artificial flowers or colourful paper, cut to look like flowers. The citizens start to put flowers all around, covering everywhere in flowers.

1st PLAYER   Once again they began to grow roses, bellflowers...
2nd PLAYER   Violets, daffodils...
1st PLAYER   Daisies, day lilies...
2nd PLAYER   Clivias, begonias...
1st PLAYER   Azaleas, camellias...
2nd PLAYER   Water lilies, poppies...
1st PLAYER   Tulips and orchids.

2nd PLAYER   Everywhere is full of colourful flowers.
1st PLAYER   (*Sniffs deeply all around*) Flower smells everywhere as there used to be in the past!
2nd PLAYER   Everyone began to smile...
1st PLAYER   Everyone was happy again....
2nd PLAYER   Flowers blossomed...
1st PLAYER   The sun rose and the sun set. The moon rose and the moon set. The sun and the moon followed one another...
2nd PLAYER   The water flowed. Days passed...
1st PLAYER   At last, it was the harvest season.

Citizens come up onto the stage with bunches of flowers in their hands, flower necklaces on their necks, flower bracelets on their arms. It is full of flowers everywhere.

2nd PLAYER   The harvest season for the flowers. Time to pick them...
1st PLAYER   The harvest time for the flowers. Time to make jam, cookies, and medication out of them...
2nd PLAYER   So, the harvest time for the flowers...
1st PLAYER   So, the time for Princess Flower and Prince Flower to get married...
2nd PLAYER   So, the time for the wedding. Time for the feast. Time to dance. Time to play.

The musicians start to play a joyful, rhythmic melody. A

young woman and a young man dance at the front of the stage in such a way as to reflect the equality and balance of the Land of Flowers.

1st PLAYER	King Flower and Queen Flower kept their promise.
2nd PLAYER	In the flower harvest season, they made preparations for the marriage of Prince Flower and Princess Flower.

Everyone starts to help Prince Flower and Princess Flower prepare as if they are going to dance. Both are decorated with flowers. They dress both of them in flowery outfits. They prepare horse Begonia and horse Benny at either side of the stage. They cover them in flowers.

1st PLAYER	Everyone did their best to make it a beautiful wedding ceremony...
2nd PLAYER	All the flower citizens attended the wedding ceremony...
1st PLAYER	And King Bluebell, the old King of the Land of Flowers, caused a great surprise.

King Bluebell, Queen Rose and the guards come on-stage, accompanied by drum and trumpet sounds. Everyone applauds and cheers. Drums and trumpets accompany the cheering. Begonia and Benny accompany them by neighing happily.

EVERYONE	Long live King Flower! Long live our King Bluebell! Long live King Flower! May he live long!
KING F.	My dear flower people. I am very

	happy, today. Our land turned into a desert because the flowers faded and died. This courageous, wise, kind-hearted and beautiful daughter of mine, the Flower Princess, managed to bring us new seeds, overcoming all obstacles. Our Land is full of flowers, again. We are the Land of Flowers, again. I am glad to marry her to the hard-working, skilful and handsome Prince Flower whom she loves, now, in this harvest season.
EVERYONE	Long live Princess Flower! Long live Princess Flower! Long live Princess Flower! May she live long!
KING F.	As for me, my dear flower citizens. I am very old. I can not fully manage to rule the Land of Flowers. It would be better if a young and wise King ruled our Land. That's why I would like to hand over my role as monarch to my daughter Princess Lily, who has proved what a skilful, successful, and kind-hearted person she is. I'd like to place my crown on her head. If you all accept this, Princess Lily will be your Queen Flower from now on.

EVERYONE   Long live Princess Flower! Long live Princess Flower! Long live Princess Flower! May she live long!

The King takes off his crown and places it on the head of Princess Flower. He kisses her on the forehead. Princess Flower hugs her mother. Her mother kisses her. Everybody applauds, cheering. Benny and Begonia accompany them, neighing happily.

EVERYONE   Long live Princess Flower! Long live Princess Flower! Long live Princess Flower! May she live long!
PRINCESS F.   Dear mother and father... Dear citizens of the Land of Flowers... Thank you very much for accepting me as the new queen of the Land of Flowers.

Applause and cheers. Begonia and Benny accompany them, neighing happily.

PRINCESS F.   But we have had a painful experience. The results of what men do without women can be very terrible. Similarly, the things that women do without men may not be that good. So, I would like to rule the Land of Flowers with Prince Flower, my husband-to-be. As women and men are expected to work together, we should also rule the country together.

Everybody, including King Bluebell and Queen Rose, applauds. The people cheer. Benny and Begonia accompany them, neighing happily.

EVERYONE	Long live Queen Flower! Long live King Flower!
KING F.	I heartily appreciate this wise proposal. I congratulate the new King and the Queen joyfully.
EVERYONE	Long live Queen Flower! Long live King Flower!
PRINCE F.	Thank you very much for accepting me as your King… We will rule our beautiful land together in equality…
PRINCESS F.	Our men and women will all be equal…. We will do everything together….
EVERYONE	Long live our new Queen Flower! Long live our new King Flower! Long live women and men! Long live equality! Long live….
KING F.	Now, let's celebrate this together. Let's dance together. Let's sing. Let's have fun. Let the music play. Let the dance start!

Music starts. Everybody gathers around the bride and the groom. Soon, guards bring a new crown on a cushion. The King places the crown on Princess Flower's head. Everybody applauds and cheers. Princess Flower and Prince Flower kiss each other and begin to dance. King

Bluebell and Queen Rose dance also. The people of the Land of Flowers dance in couples. The 1st PLAYER and the 2nd PLAYER are now one of the happy couples in the Land of Flowers.

The music changes. Begonia and Benny, who were positioned at one side of the stage, are brought forward. Princess Flower rides on Benny, the male horse, whose body is played by a female PLAYER, and Prince Flower rides on the female horse, Begonia, whose body is played by a male PLAYER. Begonia and Benny give the appearance of another couple who will share life together from now on.

Accompanied by the new music, the other couples walk and dance hand-in-hand following the soon-to-be King Flower and Queen Flower who ride on Begonia and Benny. They walk around the stage, singing and dancing rhythmically.)

THE SONG OF THE HAPPY LAND OF FLOWERS

Together, men and women,
We'll grow beautiful flowers
And lead happy lives
In our flowery land.

When the song is finished, the music stops. Every-one remains motionless. Then the internal play ends.

THE EPILOGUE

Each actor steps out of his or her role, removes some of their costume and accessories, and takes a place on the stage. They start a modern dance as PLAYERS, as women and men. They sing the last song of the play together.

EPILOGUE SONG

If only the tales were plays,
If only the plays were real,
If only the realities of life,
Were as lovely as tales

Our play is over now.
We hope your life is full of play.
Let this play be
A gift from us to you

When the song and the dance are over, the PLAYERS greet the audience. This greeting should be in couples, in a woman-man order.

THE END

HASAN ERKEK is a playwright, poet and professor of drama. He has published 25 artistic and academic books in twelve different countries and has received more than eighteen prizes. His published academic work focuses on the art of drama, while both his academic and creative work has a strong focus on theatre for children.

His plays have been performed at more than 38 theatres including Turkish National Theatres and six in other countries. Approximately twenty of his radio plays have been broadcast by national radio stations in Turkey. Some of his film scripts have been filmed.

Hasan Erkek has taken part and presented papers in many international theatre festivals, and more than a hundred of his articles have been published in various journals and newspapers. He has given courses in various faculties on play-reading, dramaturgy, dramatisation, creative writing, drama techniques and contemporary theatre

Hasan Erkek has served as an Executive Board Member and Vice-president in ASSITEJ Turkey, as the president of Turkish Playwrights and Play Translators Association and as the Head of the Department of Performing Arts at Anadolu University.

PLEASE WRITE TO US!

Princess Flower
is the first English translation of a play originally written and performed in Turkish in Turkey.

We are interested to read your comments on this play by Hasan Erkek.

Write to our email address,
info@proversepublishing.com,
giving us a few sentences
which you are willing for us to publish,
describing your response to this book.

If your comments are chosen to be included
in our E-Newsletter or website,
we will select another title published by Proverse
and send you a complimentary copy.

When you write to us, please include your name,
email address and correspondence address.

Unless you state otherwise, we will assume that we may cut or edit your comments for publication.

We will use your initials to attribute your comments.

SOME EDUCATIONAL BOOKS PUBLISHED BY PROVERSE HONG KONG

POEMS TO ENJOY, BOOK 1
Edited by Verner Bickley. Book 1 of a 5-volume graded series. HK & UK: 2012. Pbk. 136 pp. (inc. *c.*35 b/w original line-drawings & Teacher's and Student's Notes). With audio CDs. ISBN 978-988-8167-54-8.

POEMS TO ENJOY, BOOK 2
Edited by Verner Bickley. Book 2 of a 5-volume graded series. HK & UK: 2013. Pbk. 136pp. (inc. *c.*37 b/w original line-drawings & Teacher's and Student's Notes). With audio CDs. ISBN 978-988-8167-51-7.

POEMS TO ENJOY, BOOK 3
Edited by Verner Bickley. Book 3 of a 5-volume graded series. HK & UK: 2013. Pbk. 166pp. (inc. *c.*39 b/w original line-drawings & Teacher's and Student's Notes). w. audio CDs. ISBN 978-988-19934-1-0.

POEMS TO ENJOY, BOOK 4
Edited by Verner Bickley. Book 4 of a 5-volume graded series. HK & UK: 2013. Pbk. 200 pp. (inc. *c.*41 b/w original line-drawings & Teacher's and Student's Notes). With audio CDs. ISBN 978-988-8167-50-0.

POEMS TO ENJOY, BOOK 5
Edited by Verner Bickley. Book 5 of a 5-volume graded series. HK & UK: 2013. Pbk. 192pp. (inc. *c.*36 b/w original line-drawings & Teacher's and Student's Notes). With audio CDs. ISBN 978-988-8167-49-4.

FIND OUT MORE ABOUT OUR AUTHORS, BOOKS, EVENTS AND THE INTERNATIONAL PROVERSE PRIZE
for unpublished fiction, non-fiction or poetry.

Visit our website
http://www.proversepublishing.com

Visit our distributor's website
<www.chineseupress.com>

Follow us on Twitter
Follow news and conversation: <twitter.com/Proversebooks>
OR
Copy and paste the following to your browser window and follow the instructions: https://twitter.com/#!/ProverseBooks

"Like" us on www.facebook.com/ProversePress

Request our free E-Newsletter
Send your request to info@proversepublishing.com.

Availability
Most titles are available in Hong Kong and world-wide from our Hong Kong based Distributor, The Chinese University Press of Hong Kong, The Chinese University of Hong Kong, Shatin, NT, Hong Kong SAR, China. Web: chineseupress.com

All titles are available from Proverse Hong Kong and the Proverse Hong Kong UK-based Distributor.

We have stock-holding retailers in Hong Kong, Singapore (Select Books), Canada (Elizabeth Campbell Books), Principality of Andorra (Llibreria La Puça, La Llibreria). Orders can be made from bookshops in the UK and elsewhere.

Ebooks
Most of our titles are available also as Ebooks.

www.ingramcontent.com/pod-product-compliance
Lightning Source LLC
Chambersburg PA
CBHW071121160426
43196CB00013B/2658